# FROM FARM TO FORK

# Where Does Fruit Come From?

Linda Staniford

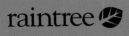

raintree

a Capstone company — publishers for children

Raintree is an imprint of Capstone Global Library Limited, a company incorporated in England and Wales having its registered office at 264 Banbury Road, Oxford, OX2 7DY – Registered company number: 6695582

www.raintree.co.uk
myorders@raintree.co.uk

Edited by Helen Cox Cannons
Designed by Steve Mead
Original illustrations © Capstone Global Library Limited 2016
Illustrated by Steve Mead
Picture research by Tracy Cummins
Production by Victoria Fitzgerald
Originated by Capstone Global Library Limited
Printed and bound in China

ISBN 978 1 4747 2123 3
20 19 18 17 16
10 9 8 7 6 5 4 3 2 1

British Library Cataloguing in Publication Data
A full catalogue record for this book is available from the British Library.

**Acknowledgements**
We would like to thank the following for permission to reproduce photographs: Alamy: foto-mix, 16, Marwood jenkins, 18; Corbis: Momatiuk - Eastcott, 9, Paulo Fridman, 15; Getty Images: Camille Tokerud, 21, ROBERT SULLIVAN/AFP, 12; iStockphoto: GeorgeDolgikh, 17; Newscom: Michele Molinari/DanitaDelimont.com, 14; Shutterstock: Africa Studio, Cover Right, 5, Alex Staroseltsev, 23 Bottom Middle, Alf Ribeiro, 8, apiguide, Cover Left, Deymos.HR, 11, EvrenKalinbacak, 19, images72, 6, Jim Parkin, Cover Back, 10, Maks Narodenko, 23 Top, 23 Top Middle, 23 Middle, Marco Ossino, 13, MO_SES Premium, 4, Tim UR, 23 Bottom, vladimir salman, 7, Voronin76, 20.

Every effort has been made to contact copyright holders of material reproduced in this book. Any omissions will be rectified in subsequent printings if notice is given to the publisher.

All the internet addresses (URLs) given in this book were valid at the time of going to press. However, due to the dynamic nature of the internet, some addresses may have changed, or sites may have changed or ceased to exist since publication. While the author and publisher regret any inconvenience this may cause readers, no responsibility for any such changes can be accepted by either the author or the publisher.

Some words are shown in bold, **like this**. You can find out what they mean by looking in the glossary.

# Contents

# What is fruit?

Fruit comes from plants. It can grow on bushes or trees. Fruit is the part of the plant that contains seeds. Seeds make new plants.

Fruit is an important part of our diet.
The fruit we eat gives us **vitamins**.
Vitamins keep our bodies healthy.

# Where does fruit grow?

Fruit grows all over the world. Fruit can be grown on large or small farms. Some fruit grows in **orchards**.

You can even grow some kinds of fruit yourself. In this book we will look at how oranges get from farms to your plate.

# How are oranges planted?

Oranges grow on trees. The trees start their life as seeds, known as pips. The seeds are planted in pots. Orange trees then grow from these seeds.

When the orange trees have grown big enough, they are planted in an **orchard**. It can take around five years before they have oranges growing on them.

# How do oranges grow?

In spring, orange trees grow flowers called **blossom**. The blossom smells sweet and attracts insects.

The blossom dies and falls off the trees.
Fruits grow instead. They are small and
green at first, but get bigger and turn
orange as they **ripen**.

# How are oranges harvested?

When the oranges are **ripe**, they are **harvested**. Harvesting means picking a crop. Sometimes a machine is used to shake the trees. This makes the oranges fall off into a big tray.

Most oranges are harvested by hand.
Harvesters climb ladders, pick the
oranges and put them into sacks
or crates.

# What happens after harvesting?

After they have been **harvested**, the oranges are sorted by machine. Any oranges that are not suitable for eating are taken out. Then the oranges are washed.

Some oranges are used to make fruit juice. These oranges are taken to factories. There, the oranges are peeled and squeezed to get the juice out.

# How are oranges preserved?

**Preserving** is treating the fruit to stop it from going bad. Marmalade is a kind of preserve. It is like jam, but made from oranges.

The peel of the orange is used as well as the insides. The peel makes marmalade taste bitter. Sugar is added to sweeten it. Some types of orange can also be preserved in cans.

# What happens to oranges after washing?

The oranges are packed in boxes and loaded onto lorries. The lorries take some of the oranges to shops and markets.

Others are taken to ports where they are loaded onto **cargo** ships. The ships take the oranges all over the world. They go to countries where oranges cannot grow.

# How do the oranges get to our table?

Shop workers put the oranges out on shelves in the shops. They are ready for us to eat. There are a lot of other fruits in the shops as well.

When we go grocery shopping we choose our oranges. The oranges have had a long journey from farm to fork!

# All kinds of fruit!

There are many kinds of fruit. Some fruit only grows in hot countries. For example, mangoes grow in India and bananas grow in the Caribbean. Other fruit, such as apples and pears, grow in cooler places.

You can eat the seeds of some fruit, but not stones. Peaches have stones inside and we do not eat them. Strawberries have seeds on the outside. We eat them.

# Glossary

**blossom**  flower or flowers on a bush or tree

**cargo**  objects carried by a ship, aircraft or other vehicle

**harvest**  pick a crop

**orchard**  field or farm where fruit trees are grown

**preserve**  keep something fresh. Fruit that has been made into jam or marmalade is called preserve.

**ripe**  ready to pick and eat

**vitamins**  good things in foods that help our bodies stay healthy

# Find out more

## Books

*Apples Grow on Trees* (What Grows in My Garden), Anne
  Rooney (QEB Publishing, 2012)
*Food from Farms* (World of Farming), Nancy Dickmann
  (Raintree, 2010)

## Websites

**https://learnenglishkids.britishcouncil.org/en/
category/topics/food**

This website contains lots of fun, food-based games for
you to play.

# Index